Financial Guidance
for
IT Professionals

Rajiv Prabhakar

First printing: 2024

ISBN: 9798884840249

British Cataloguing Publication Data:
A catalogue record of this book is available from The British Library.

"When I was young, I thought that money was the most important thing in life. Now that I am old, I know that it is."

Oscar Wilde

Contents

Chapter 1: Introduction

IT professionals are great at solving problems. They have the skills to find ways to do things better and more efficiently. But that doesn't mean they have all the answers.

I've been a financial adviser for over 15 years, specialising in helping IT professionals plan their finances. In my experience, despite their skills in fixing problems, one challenge many of them struggle with is financial planning. Why? Largely because hectic work and personal lives mean they often don't find the time to get their financial affairs in order. A lack of easy-to-understand, easily available information is also part of the problem.

My job is to help my clients achieve financial wellbeing. This means different things to different people, but for me it's about knowing what you want to achieve with your money, now and in the future, and having the plans in place to reach those goals. It's about feeling confident and in control.

Feeling comfortable about your finances has obvious mental health benefits. On the flipside, poor financial wellbeing is a well-documented cause of stress, particularly in the current financial climate.

It has given me enormous personal and professional satisfaction to see my clients achieving their financial goals over the years. It's been a privilege to meet people from all walks of life and gain an even deeper appreciation of the excellent work they do serving the community.

I've been encouraged to write this book mainly by my clients, with the aim of providing jargon-free guidance on the key areas of financial planning for IT professionals.

It's not intended as a DIY guide. When it comes to successful financial planning, the value of professional advice cannot be underestimated. IT professionals understand that to solve a problem you need to ask the right questions. It's the role of a financial adviser to ask the sometimes difficult questions that need to be answered to uncover what's really worrying people when it comes to their finances. Only then can a plan be put in place to ease those concerns and put them on the path to true financial security.

The tailored advice I provide my clients is based on a thorough understanding of their needs and aspirations. I pride myself on the trusted, long-term relationships I build with them, which provide the foundations for regular reviews that take place to keep their plans on track as circumstances change.

What I wanted to do in writing this book was help build a better understanding of financial jargon and products, so readers can be better informed and more confident around money – and, as a result, manage their wealth better.

I'd also like this book to be a way of helping others learn. I will be donating a portion of the proceeds from the sales of this book to two of my favourite charities in India, both of which help underprivileged children with their education.

Aahar focuses on providing essential infrastructure for primary schools in villages in the south of India. The charity aims to break the generational cycle of poverty by bringing care, education and opportunity to some of India's most vulnerable children.

The Swami Vivekananda Youth Movement (SVYM) has been working for nearly four decades to help indigenous and rural people in southern India. The organisation has its headquarters in the Mysuru district of Karnataka state and focuses on health, education, socio-economic empowerment and training and research.

Chapter 2:
Why IT Professionals?

When I set out as a financial adviser, I was very fortunate that several of my friends worked in IT and came from my home country, India. That provided me with a good client base to begin my new career, which I was then able to develop through recommendations and referrals to others working in the industry.

Naturally, I've met and worked with clients at different stages of their career and been on hand when needed as they've experienced the full range of life events.

Of course, every client is different, but I've found there are several common factors when it comes to their objectives, priorities and challenges.

The main problem is a lack of time. They are trying to juggle family responsibilities and other outside activities with very busy professional lives. In short, they struggle to balance life and work effectively.

This means they have little time to focus on their finances other than to prioritise paying off their mortgage debt. When I discussed their financial goals, there was often very low awareness about how to plan and achieve their future financial objectives.

Whilst my clients rarely have a plan of action to achieve them, my conversations usually reveal some common themes in terms of priorities:

- Achieving future financial security
- Protecting their families in the event of serious illness or premature death
- Providing for children's school fees and saving for higher education
- Paying off debt

Naturally, the importance and priority of these goals changes at different life stages. Every client's situation is unique and requires different solutions, but to illustrate how needs change over the years let's use the example of Amber and his wife Abhi, who work in IT and legal professions.

Late-20s to mid-30s

Their priority is saving for a deposit to purchase their first property. They're also planning for when they want to start a family, so the costs of childcare and nursery education need to be considered.

In addition to these savings needs, they should ensure they have an adequate emergency fund to cover any break in employment, ill health, or unforeseen expenses. I would also encourage them to start laying the foundations for their future financial security by starting to save regularly in tax-efficient investments such as an ISA or a personal pension. There is no magic formula to achieving long-term financial security; it's about saving as much as you can, for as long as you can.

They need to ensure they have valid and up-to-date Wills in place and should also consider putting Powers of Attorney in place to protect their welfare and finances in case they are unable to act for themselves.

Mid-30s to 50s

They have purchased a property and are settled into jobs with good incomes. Their children are in full-time education. Their priorities include reducing their mortgage debt, but they also need to have adequate life cover in place to ensure the mortgage is protected and can be paid off should the worst happen.

With a growing family, they also need to consider other areas of protection, such as critical illness cover, private medical insurance and income protection.

They enjoy good holidays and are also looking at planning for private school fees. As their disposable income increases, they should look to boost savings into tax-efficient wrappers such as ISAs, pensions and investment bonds.

They should also consider options to save tax-efficiently for the children, to help meet the future costs of further education, first home deposits and so on. A Junior ISA is an ideal vehicle into which other family and friends can also contribute.

50s to retirement

They have well-established careers at peak earnings levels. They want to pay off the mortgage and reduce other debts to save on interest payments. The cost of children's university fees and marriage need to be planned for.

This is the last opportunity to ensure savings are in place to fund the best possible retirement lifestyle, which means maximising investment into ISAs, pensions and, potentially, other tax-advantaged products.

In retirement, it's about having sufficient income from pensions and other investments to enjoy life to the full.

Estate planning becomes a priority, protecting wealth from Inheritance Tax for the benefit of future generations and creating a legacy by reviewing Wills and other plans. This may involve lifetime gifting and the use of trusts.

Chapter 3: Steps to Successful Financial Planning

What is financial planning? To me, it's the process through which you organise your finances in a way that enables you to navigate the challenges and needs at each stage of your life, and which makes you feel in control.

There is no 'one-size-fits-all' solution to successful financial planning. Every person is different, and every financial plan needs to be personal, tailored to their specific needs and attitudes.

Whilst everyone's financial plan will be unique, the key steps to creating a successful one are consistent. Done well, it is a process that builds long-term, trusted relationships between a financial adviser and their client.

Step 1 – Understand who and where you are

'Know your client' is a key mantra for a financial adviser. We can only provide the best advice if we thoroughly understand our client. It's about more than just money. It's about your family, your work, what stage you're at in life, your overall approach and attitude to your finances, your interests and so on.

But I find that this 'discovery' stage often has real value for my clients, too. The factfinding process draws out questions that you may not have asked yourself, and the answers reveal something to you as well as to your adviser. Some of it might be challenging and a little bit uncomfortable. It's the job of your adviser to make you think about things you may not have considered. The soft facts about you and your attitudes, and the hard facts, like how much money you've got in the bank, are equally as important in creating your financial plan.

Step 2 – Understand your financial position

Just like a business, individuals have assets and liabilities, income and expenditure. Getting an in-depth assessment of your personal balance sheet is arguably the most important part of the planning process.

Your assets include your cash savings, investments and pension savings, and property. Liabilities will include long-term debt, such as a mortgage, as well as any short-term borrowing through credit cards and overdrafts.

Household income includes regular earnings and is likely to fluctuate, particularly if you're self-employed, but also due to dividends and bonuses, so it's important to get an accurate picture. Expenditure will be a combination of outgoings that have to be paid, such as utility bills and mortgage payments, as well as discretionary spending on holidays, hobbies and so on.

Step 3 – Establish your goals

What do you want to achieve with your wealth? The next stage in the planning process is to determine your financial goals and targets.

At one level, it could be ensuring that your family is fully protected should you die or suffer a serious illness. But your future view could well include when you plan or expect to retire, ambitions for putting your children through private education, paying off the mortgage early, buying a holiday home, how much you'd like to travel in retirement, and so on.

Of course, plans and circumstances do change. The receipt of a windfall, such as an inheritance, could shift the timescales for certain goals. No one knows what's around the corner, but setting out your financial aims provides the foundations on which to build your plan.

Step 4 – Understand your attitude to risk

If you're to achieve your longer-term financial goals, you'll need to give your money the chance to grow. That means taking some risk, because leaving your money in cash won't maintain or increase its future spending power.

Most people appreciate that the potential to achieve greater rewards goes in hand in hand with taking more risk. But how comfortable are you taking risks with the money you invest? The answer to that question could easily change depending on where you are on your financial journey.

When you're younger, you may be willing and able to accept more risk, knowing that time is on your side to recover any losses and hopefully achieve the greater returns on offer. But as you get older, perhaps approaching or in retirement, you may feel less able to absorb short-term losses and more worried about keeping the value of your retirement pot intact.

That's why a key step in the financial planning process is to understand how much investment risk you can tolerate. What is the appropriate level of risk that will give you a chance of achieving your goals, whilst not causing you to lose sleep at night? If stock markets fall, would your automatic reaction be to run for the hills or consider investing more money while prices are depressed?

The answers to these and many other questions will help shape your financial plan.

Step 5 – Create your plan

Once you've gone through the steps of understanding where you are now and where you want to be in the future, the next stage is to work out how to join those two points and what the staging posts need to be along the way.

Cashflow modelling is a way of projecting future income and expenditure to show what money is required year by year and how this will be funded. Using such tools can highlight any future shortfalls and show what level of returns you need from your investments.

Another method is to capitalise your future expenditure to calculate the capital lump sum you'll need to create the level of annual income you want in retirement, for example. Your plan then needs to build that capital value over the time period available.

It's also important that your forward-looking plan builds in regular checkpoints to give you an accurate picture of whether you're on target and what might need to change in order to make sure you reach your end goal.

Step 6 – Implement your plan

It's now time to put your plan into effect. For each section – which might include pensions, investing, protection, tax and estate planning – the next stage is to select the right products, investment funds, tax wrappers and so on.

This is the actual structure of your financial plan, which should define how much is to be invested in which area, the returns needed, and the benchmarks against which progress is to be measured.

Step 7 – Review and renew your plan

Successful financial planning is an ongoing process. Reaching your financial goals in life is not something that can be achieved with one meeting or one plan.

That's because things change. The future is uncertain. The economic environment can significantly change the outlook, as we've seen recently with inflation surging and interest rates being hiked from record low levels. Economic factors can hugely influence how investments perform, which might be differently to expectations.

But, most crucially, your own circumstances and priorities will change over the years, in ways that often can't be foreseen. Marriage, divorce, ill health, changes to your employment situation, problems with your business and unplanned expenses are just some of the events that can move the goalposts and affect your future plans.

That's why regular reviews are vital to achieving long-term financial success. You should aim to review progress against your plan at least once a year, but more frequently if there are significant changes to your situation.

Not everything will need adjusting. Some parts of your plan will be multi-year objectives that need time to come to fruition. Others may need to be adapted if they're not working or if your needs have changed.

Regular reviews provide peace of mind that your financial plans are being looked after, helping you feel in control and more confident about the future.

Chapter 4: Investment Planning

Why do we need to invest our money? It's a question I'm often asked when I meet prospective clients for the first time. They say they're not risk takers and worry about losing all their money. Or they believe investing in the stock market is only for wealthy people who can afford to gamble with their savings.

Investing is not without risk, yet there is also a risk in leaving your money in cash. There are three main reasons why investing is a good thing to do:

- To give your money the chance to grow.
- To help generate an income.
- To help counter the impact of inflation on the spending power of your money.

Before expanding on those reasons, it's important to emphasise the vital role that cash plays in your overall financial planning strategy. It is the right place to hold funds you might need in the short term, or to cover emergency, unforeseen expenses. I always recommend my clients hold enough in easily accessible savings to meet 3-6 months' worth of expenses, but it is often more than that. In short, hold enough money in cash that makes you feel comfortable and means you can sleep well at night.

The key thing to avoid is having to dip into your investment pot to meet those short-term expenses. This can prove particularly costly if you have to withdraw funds during periods of stock market volatility, when prices are down. The funds you commit to your longer-term financial goals should be 'five years and forget it' money, at the very least.

Of course, it's worth shopping around to find the best cash rates you can, but savers are all too aware of the low cash returns on offer in recent years; interest rates have typically failed to keep pace with inflation.

That's why cash isn't the solution to achieving long-term financial security. To reach your bigger financial goals, you need to invest rather than save. You need to take more risk.

Grow your money

The more risk you are prepared to take, the greater the potential rewards. What's true for investments is also true for our careers and many other aspects of life.

In a bank account, your capital is secure because it is not exposed to market volatility. On the flipside, it has little scope to grow, particularly in recent years when interest rates have been so low.

There is a risk when you invest in the stock market and other assets. Values can, and do, go down as well as up. That's why it's vital you take a long-term view of investing, and don't panic when markets fluctuate in the short term. But over the long term, investors will only continue to commit their money if they receive sufficient reward for taking those risks, compared to the return they could get from risk-free assets. This is called the equity risk premium. Without it, stock markets wouldn't work.

Another reason to invest is to give yourself the chance to benefit from compound growth – something Albert Einstein is said to have called 'the eighth wonder of the world'. When you invest your money, it hopefully earns returns, and then those returns can also generate returns of their own. Over time, this 'snowball effect' can significantly boost your capital.

The potential for compounding growth is why I encourage clients to begin their investing journey as soon as possible, even if it's a small amount to begin with. Investing is a long game – the more time you give your money to grow, the more you stand to benefit from compounding returns.

Generate an income

Most of us invest with a view to one day taking an income from the money we've saved up, usually when we retire. We want to ensure we've got as large a pension pot as possible, enabling us to live the lifestyle we've dreamt of and worked so hard for.

When you invest your money, you have the potential to generate returns from two sources. In addition to the scope for the capital value to increase over time, many types of investments generate a natural income. Each year, companies pay out a proportion of profits as dividends to shareholders. Commercial property receives rental income from tenants. Bonds make regular interest payments.

This contrasts with holding money in cash, where the capital is secure, but the only element of return is the interest paid.

This can create a 'vicious circle' when the time comes to draw an income. As inflation erodes the spending power of their interest, savers are obliged to top up the interest payments with capital from their deposit. Of course, this has the effect of further reducing the income in the following year, necessitating a further withdrawal of capital, and so on.

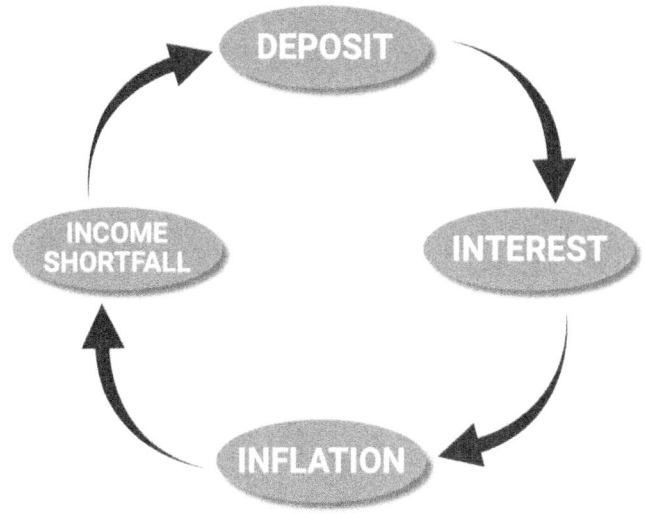

Over the longer term, the income generated from an investment portfolio makes up a significant proportion of the overall return. If you're still earning and don't need to spend your investment income, reinvesting it back into your investment can provide a significant boost over time by adding to the potential for compound growth mentioned previously.

Combat inflation

The last two decades have, until recently, been an era of record low interest rates that have failed to match even relatively low levels of inflation. As a result, most cash savings have been losing value in real terms.

Even at low levels, inflation has a corrosive effect on the value of your money. An inflation rate of just 3% would halve the spending power of your savings in 24 years. That's why building your retirement pot, and other long-term objectives, needs a different solution to leaving your money in cash.

Investing in assets such as stocks, bonds and property has a great track record of providing inflation-beating returns over the medium to long term. To meet your longer-term financial goals, you need your money to not just maintain its value but have the potential to grow in value as well.

One way I convey the difference between investing in cash and other assets is to use the example of what happens to the money held in a bank or building society. Someone depositing £25,000 in a savings account ten years ago would have received regular interest payments, which, over the years, are unlikely to go up or down very much. Today, because of inflation, that income now buys much less in real terms, plus the real value of the original deposit is also well down.

In the meantime, it's likely that £25,000 deposit was lent to someone else who used it to buy a house. The value of that house has almost certainly increased over those ten years, probably at a faster rate than inflation.

While the saver has experienced diminishing returns in real terms, the borrower has enjoyed real capital growth. The choice for cash savers is whether to leave all their money on deposit working for someone else, or put it to work for themselves by investing in assets that offer the potential for real growth.

--

When I talk to clients about investing, I spend a lot of time getting a thorough understanding of their attitude to risk and reward. Without it, we cannot create the right investment strategy.

This is where professional advice comes into its own. Getting it wrong increases the likelihood of disappointment or distress further down the line, if investors don't achieve the returns they'd anticipated, or they panic when markets fall.

I'm always keen to find out about their previous experience of investing and how they would react if markets went up or down. To achieve better returns over the medium to long term, they must be able to withstand short-term volatility and stay invested.

The press is always keen to highlight days when billions of pounds are wiped off the value of shares but you don't often see headlines about the good days on stock markets. Often, the very best days follow sharp falls, which is why I stress the importance of not being influenced by short-term falls and negative coverage. The worst thing you can do as an investor is to make knee-jerk sell decisions when markets have a bad day.

When it comes to investing, doing nothing is often the best course of action.

Investing tax-efficiently

The first step to creating the right investment strategy is putting together a portfolio that matches your risk profile and objectives. Next is ensuring that your investments are held in the appropriate tax wrappers, to suit your individual circumstances and to give your money the best possible chance of maximising returns through tax efficiency.

It's important that the tax tail doesn't wag the dog when it comes to your investment strategy. But, over the long term, having your money sheltered in the right tax wrappers can significantly boost the value of the funds you're relying on to secure your financial future.

The most well-known and well-used tax-efficient wrappers are pensions and Individual Savings Accounts (ISAs). Despite this, I am often asked to explain more about ISAs.

ISAs

Since their introduction in 1999, Individual Savings Accounts (ISAs) have proved one of the most popular ways to save and invest. Broadly, there are two types: Cash ISAs and Stocks & Shares ISAs.

You can save £20,000 into ISAs each tax year, but this annual allowance cannot be carried forward, so if you don't use it, you lose it. Previously, it was only possible to subscribe to one ISA of each type in a tax year, but from April 2024 you can make multiple subscriptions to the same-type ISA in the same tax year. You must be over 18 and a UK resident for tax purposes. Once your money is held in an ISA, you won't pay any more tax on income or capital gains, making it a great way to invest for the future.

In the Spring Budget in 2024, plans were announced for a new British ISA, which would increase the annual allowance by £5,000 where the additional investment was made solely into UK assets. However, at the time of publication further information and the launch date had not been confirmed.

Often, I find people are only aware of Cash ISAs, which account for over three-quarters of all ISA subscriptions. A Cash ISA is simply a deposit savings account that pays tax-free interest.

What savers often overlook is that they also have a Personal Savings Allowance, which enables basic-rate and higher-rate taxpayers to earn annual interest of £1,000 and £500 respectively from standard cash accounts before any tax is deducted.

Of course, with a Cash ISA, all your interest will remain tax-free. That's great, but there is a risk that savers don't make the most of their valuable ISA allowance because the real returns (after inflation) are still low, which means they're not maximising the tax breaks on offer.

I often find that clients have money saved in Cash ISAs for many years, usually because "it's safe". But doing so means that cash has become part of their long-term investment strategy, rather than being the right home for the 'emergency funds' they might need in the next few years.

It's worth noting that Cash ISAs are covered by the Financial Services Compensation Scheme (FSCS). In common with other bank accounts held with UK-authorised banks and building societies, if a firm fails the FSCS protects and compensates up to £85,000 per person, per bank or building society.

As the name suggests, a Stocks & Shares ISA can invest in a wide range of stock market and other investments. Most ISA providers allow you to invest lump sums or make regular payments.

Regular saving is a great way to invest for the future because it instils a discipline to put money away, regardless of what stock markets are doing from one day to the next. It removes the worry some investors have about investing at the 'wrong time', i.e. just before markets take a fall.

Regular saving is a tried and trusted way to help control risk over the longer term. Short-term volatility is an inherent feature of investing in the stock market, but through regular saving it's possible to make market volatility work to your advantage.

By drip-feeding your money into the market, you have the potential to buy more units or shares when prices are falling. Of course, no one can predict when it will be, but when prices recover you'll have more units with a higher value.

Saving regularly or phasing a lump sum investment from cash into the market over a number of months makes it possible to benefit from the short-term ups and downs and, at the very least, reduce the worry of investing at the wrong time.

As mentioned before, it's critical that investors take a long-term view and avoid the temptation to 'play the market'.

Often, the best days for markets follow very closely behind the bad ones, which is why I stress to my clients the dangers of trying to time the market. Time in, not timing, is the key to investment success.

A Stocks & Shares ISA provides scope to benefit from both income and capital growth from the underlying investments. Your money is sheltered from Income Tax and Capital Gains Tax (CGT) and recent tax changes have made this benefit even more valuable, which is why making the most of your annual ISA allowance is so important.

For assets held outside of products like ISAs and pensions, investors have an annual CGT allowance – the amount of profit that can be made before tax is payable. In the 2023/24 tax year, the allowance was cut from £12,300 to £6,000, and it will be halved again to £3,000 from April 2024.

If you don't make full use of your CGT allowance in a given tax year you aren't allowed to carry it forward to the next.

These cuts mean that taxpayers who have historically used their CGT allowance each year via share dealing will find it increasingly difficult to extract funds from their investment portfolio in a tax-efficient way. It also creates a bigger CGT risk for those selling second homes or buy-to-let properties, selling a business or disposing of other valuable assets.

The government has also cut the Dividend Allowance, which enables investors to receive annual tax-free dividend income. This allowance dropped from £2,000 to £1,000 in April 2023, and will be cut again to £500 in April 2024.

All this means that ISAs (and pensions) have an even more important role to play in helping create tax-efficient funds for your future financial security.

Junior ISA

Launched back in 2011 to replace the less successful Child Trust Funds, Junior ISAs are an increasingly popular way for parents (and other relatives) to build up tax-efficient funds for young people faced with future financial challenges such as getting on the property ladder and higher education costs.

The tax breaks are the same as for an adult ISA, and there is a generous annual allowance of £9,000. The child must be under 18 and a UK resident. The account can only be opened by a parent or guardian, but anyone can contribute to it.

When the child turns 18, the Junior ISA is converted to an adult ISA and they can access the funds at this point.

Parents have the same choice of a Stocks & Shares or Cash Junior ISA. Despite this being a long-term savings opportunity, over half of Junior ISA subscriptions are made into the cash option. As with adult ISAs, this means many parents may not be making the most of the chance to build capital for their children.

I'm always keen for parents and grandparents to consider Junior ISAs as part of the financial plans for their family. It helps teach children about the importance of money and saving, and contributions to a Junior ISA are an ideal way to use gifting allowances for estate planning.

Unit Trusts

Don't put all your eggs in one basket. Diversification is one of my golden rules of investing. The wider you can spread your investments, the more you can reduce your risk. Diversifying your money across lots of different investments may mean they're not all going up in value at the same time, but equally, they are unlikely to all fall in value either. It gives you the potential to capture investment returns from as many sources as possible.

Unit trusts are an ideal solution to diversify your portfolio and benefit from expert investment management. A unit trust is a collective investment vehicle, which is a complicated way of saying that your money is pooled with that of thousands of other investors into one fund. That provides the manager of the fund with the ability to invest in different asset classes (equities, bonds, property, commodities and so on) across different geographic areas in a wide number of companies and sectors (pharmaceuticals, IT, industrials, utilities, etc.).

Unit trusts typically specialise in certain asset classes or geographic areas, so a blend of different funds can provide investors with a balanced and diverse portfolio, tailored to their particular risk profile.

For example, emerging markets can be a volatile area for investing. That may suit younger investors who have time on their side to ride out the ups and downs; however, older investors may not be willing or able to accept the fluctuations in value.

You can normally invest in unit trusts with a lump sum or through regular savings. As with all stock market-based investments, unit trusts should only be considered as options for the medium to long term, i.e. at least five years.

The advantages of unit trusts mean they are very commonly the underlying investments used in Stocks & Shares ISAs, combining tax efficiency with expert fund management. It is possible to invest a Stocks & Shares ISA in the shares of one, or a few, individual companies, but that increases risk considerably, which is why I encourage my clients to adopt a very diversified strategy that encapsulates possibly hundreds of different companies.

Investment Bonds

Investment bonds are another solution for investing a lump sum for the medium to long term. An investment bond is a single premium life insurance policy, and it is their tax treatment which makes them particularly useful for trust and estate planning.

Tax on income and gains is accounted for within the fund, which makes investment bonds flexible and administratively simple. There are two types of investment bond: onshore and offshore. The main difference between them is in how they are taxed, and the suitability will depend on the current and future tax status of the investor, so getting professional advice is vital.

Just like unit trusts, investors have a wide range of underlying investment funds to choose from, making it possible to create the same well-diversified portfolio, but with different tax treatment when money is withdrawn, or the investment cashed in.

--

I've talked in this section about the benefits of using professional investment managers. Alongside the importance of diversification and taking a long-term approach to investing, this is my other golden rule.

Investing in collective funds, whether through a Stocks & Shares ISA, a unit trust, or an investment bond, means your money is being looked after by a full-time expert fund manager. They will be specialists in certain areas – UK equities or commercial property, for example – and they have access to information that is simply not available to the man (or woman) on the street.

An equity manager will meet regularly with the CEOs and CFOs of the national and international companies they invest in on behalf of their clients. This provides unrivalled insight into how those companies are doing and their plans. They will have analysts studying the performance of companies they're invested in and making recommendations for new investments.

A good fund manager is not emotionally attached to the investments they make. Their objective is to maximise returns for the investors, and they are remunerated based on their performance.

I see my role as working in tandem with the professionals managing my clients' funds. My job is to help clients plan and manage their finances, being there for them on a day-to-day basis. That is my area of expertise. The job of the fund manager is to spend all day, every day, doing their best to ensure my clients' money is invested appropriately and with the best chance of helping them achieve their objectives. That means my clients and I can get on with doing what we're best at.

Chapter 5: Retirement Planning

Of all the topics I discuss with clients on a daily basis, pensions and planning for retirement are the issues that crop up most often.

The challenges are well known. We are living longer and healthier lives. That's great news, of course. But when retirement can potentially last 30 years or more, the risk of running out of money is a very real one for some people.

The starting point for talking to clients is to establish what retirement looks like for them. It could be about enjoying the simple things in life, or having the financial freedom to be spontaneous, to fulfil those dreams and ambitions you never had time for when you were working. Is the potential for needing to pay for future care a concern? Many will have experience from other family members of just how expensive that can be.

So, how much money will you need to live the retirement lifestyle you want? Research has shown that over three-quarters of savers don't know how much they'll need.

One thing is for sure: there is no shortcut to a comfortable retirement. It's about saving as much as you can, as soon as you can.

Starting at age 20

£725,000

Starting at age 30

£387,000

Starting at age 40

£193,000

Estimated fund size at age 68

Based on £200 invested each month, increasing by 2.5% a year:
return 5% a year, compounded monthly, after charges.
These figures are examples only and are not guaranteed.
They are not minimum or maximum amounts. What you get back
depends on how your investment grows and the tax treatment
of the investment. You could get back more or less than this.

Of course, it's all too tempting and easy to focus on immediate financial rewards or goals. After all, retirement might feel and be years away. There is a danger of telling yourself you'll start putting money away "when I can afford to" or "when I'm earning more money". The risk is leaving it too late.

As covered earlier, different ages come with different financial priorities and challenges. In your 20s, you may be more concerned about getting on the property ladder. Your 30s could be a busy time with money spent on weddings, house deposits and having children. Maybe there's a career break.

Late 40s is often when earnings peak, so you really need to take advantage of your greater financial resources. In your 50s, expenses may start to dwindle, so it's often the perfect time to catch up on saving.

Savings options such as ISAs offer real flexibility and are a great way to build wealth for the future. But a pension has one clear advantage: tax relief. If you're under 75, what you pay into a pension is boosted by 25% on day one. That's because everyone gets 20% basic rate tax relief on their pension contributions from the government.

And if you're a higher or additional rate taxpayer, you can claim even more tax relief through your annual tax return. For a higher-rate taxpayer, that means a £1 contribution into your pension is effectively costing you just 60p.

Any growth is free from Income Tax and Capital Gains Tax, which can also give your retirement fund a real boost.

The total amount that can be contributed to a pension each year, while still receiving tax relief, is called the 'annual allowance'. This includes contributions made by yourself, your employer, or anyone else. The annual allowance is currently £60,000 for most people. If your earnings are less than this, you'll be entitled to tax relief only up to the amount you earn.

However, you may be able to pay more into your pension by using unclaimed allowances for the previous three tax years. This can be a valuable opportunity to boost the size of your future retirement pot, but it's important to take advice to make sure you get it right.

It's also important to consider that pensions aren't generally counted as part of your estate for Inheritance Tax (IHT) purposes. So, saving into one will avoid IHT at 40% that your estate would be liable for if the money was held elsewhere. That can make a big difference to your plans later on.

Pension options

There are two main types of pension scheme. In a defined contribution scheme (sometimes called 'money purchase scheme'), the pension pot is based on how much is paid in. Individuals pay into a defined contribution (DC) scheme, and their employer usually will too if they've got the plan through their job.

The money paid in is invested and the size of the pension pot at the end will depend on how much has been paid in and how well the underlying investments have performed. DC plans are the most common type of pension plan nowadays. All personal pension plans and most workplace schemes are DC plans.

You can usually start taking money out of a DC plan from the age of 55, although this is rising to 57 from April 2028. There are several options for taking benefits:

- You can usually take out 25% of the amount built up as a tax-free lump sum or in stages. This might be used to pay off a mortgage or for a big-ticket purchase.
- Flexible drawdown enables you to take regular withdrawals from your plan, which can be started, stopped or changed whenever you want.

- You can take your whole pot in one go or take lots of smaller lump sums.
- You can buy a guaranteed income for life, called an annuity, that will be paid to you as long as you live.

Of course, it's very important to understand the full implications of these options, including the tax position. Making a mistake in managing your pension pot can have huge consequences.

As the name suggests, a defined benefit (or 'final salary') scheme pre-determines how much you will receive each year for life from your pension. These are usually workplace schemes set up by an employer and how much you get will depend on a number of things, such as your salary and how long you've worked for the employer.

Unlike a DC scheme, employees have little control over their pension fund. The company is responsible for the investment and bears the risk of ensuring the pot will cover the defined benefits due to the employee. The benefits are generous: typically, an inflation-linked guaranteed income until the member dies, with a surviving spouse entitled to 50% of the pension amount.

Defined benefit (DB) schemes are seen as the 'gold-plated' pension option. However, increasing life expectancy and the risks associated with providing these guarantees mean DB schemes are becoming very rare in the private sector and have been largely replaced by DC plans, placing the responsibility for saving and investing on employees.

The public sector is now the major remaining provider of DB pensions, in professions such as the NHS, teaching and the civil service.

In addition to pensions linked to your employment, there is the State Pension. Your entitlement to the State Pension depends on your National Insurance (NI) record. It can be a very useful supplement to your retirement plans, but many people don't bother to check what they're entitled to.

To be entitled to the full new State Pension of around £203.85 a week, you'll need to have made NI contributions for 35 qualifying years. You'll get a proportion of the new State Pension if you have between 10 and 35 qualifying years.

Those who have taken career breaks, brought up children, or have been self-employed may not have sufficient NI contributions to qualify for the full pension. People who miss out may be able to pay voluntary NI contributions to backfill their record and make up the difference.

It's also worth remembering that retirees can defer their State Pension and get a higher income when they claim it later in retirement. For someone who has sufficient income or savings to live off in the meantime, delaying the State Pension can be attractive because the benefits really add up.

That's because your State Pension will rise 1% for every nine weeks that you defer taking it. That works out at just under 5.8% for every full year you delay claiming.

The risk is that you don't live long enough for it to be worthwhile. Most people reaching State Pension age in good health will gain, but if you have medical problems or lower life expectancy, you may not get enough benefit.

Retirees looking to defer should always seek appropriate advice as it could affect other areas of financial planning and some other welfare benefits.

You can check your State Pension forecast using the government website: https://www.gov.uk/check-state-pension.

Pensions and IT contractors

The increase in the pension annual allowance was one of the announcements made by the government in the 2023 Budget as part of its 'Back to Work' agenda, aimed at encouraging over-50s back into work or to defer retirement.

These included the abolition of the Pension Lifetime Allowance (LTA). The LTA is the total amount you can build up in all your pension savings and still receive tax relief, which for most people is £1,073,100. Those taking benefits that exceed the LTA faced a tax charge of 55% on lump sum withdrawals and 25% if taken as a taxable income.

This charge was removed from April 2023 and the LTA abolished from April 2024.

Whilst the standard annual allowance for most people is £60,000, some additional rate taxpayers can be subject to a tapered annual allowance. The other related change in the Budget saw an increase in this allowance from £4,000 to £10,000, providing more scope for high earners to contribute to their pension.

These policies were aimed primarily at higher-earning public sector workers, particularly doctors. However, they are also of benefit to contractors working via 'inside IR35' contracts.

The IR35 or off-payroll working rules were designed to stop contractors working as 'disguised employees' and they affect all contractors who do not meet HMRC's definition of self-employed, taxing them at a rate similar to employment. The increased tax burden prompted many contractors to leave the sector and instead take on permanent roles, seek work abroad, or even retire early. This was particularly prevalent in the IT and financial services sectors.

The changes to pension allowances have led many contractors to review their position and re-enter the workforce in high-earning contract positions, even when they are inside IR35.

Those working via an umbrella company that operates a salary-sacrifice pension scheme can use this arrangement to significantly reduce their tax and National Insurance (NI) liabilities. Pension contributions made through salary sacrifice extinguish the income tax and both employer and employee NI liabilities, removing most of the additional tax burden associated with being inside IR35.

The increase in the annual allowance effectively frees up an additional £20,000 of salary that can be paid into a pension and therefore become 'tax-free'.

There are great opportunities for limited company IT contractors and umbrella employees to maximise their pension planning by making the best possible use of their annual allowances. Professional advice can help ensure that it's done properly.

Chapter 6: Protection Planning

Protection planning is not an aspirational topic – but for your family and loved ones, it could be the most important conversation you have with your adviser.

Death or serious illness aren't things we like to think about, but none of us know what the future holds. If you die or suffer a serious illness, the consequences of not having the right protection in place can be devastating. Coping without you would be tough enough for your loved ones, but what if it meant their financial security was lost too?

No amount of money can ever replace a person, but you can protect your family against those uncertainties by having the right cover in place. Knowing they will be taken care of is one thing you can then be sure about. It'll give you and them huge peace of mind.

Protection planning is a simple way to ensure they are looked after, whatever happens. Your circumstances and budget will determine the right solution for you.

Life insurance is a policy that provides a lump sum or monthly benefit if you die or become terminally ill. If people rely on you financially, or rely on your income, or if you've got any debts such as loans or mortgages, you need life cover. There are several types available to suit different situations and budgets.

Term assurance

As the name suggests, term assurance is designed to pay out a tax-free lump sum if the life assured dies within a fixed period of time. It's the most inexpensive life insurance solution, used most commonly to protect surviving family by providing the funds to pay off debts such as a mortgage. Premiums can be paid monthly or annually. If the policy doesn't pay out within the term, it lapses without any residual cash value, which is why it's the cheapest form of life cover.

Term assurance can also include terminal illness cover, which will pay out the sum assured on diagnosis of a terminal illness during the policy term. The illnesses covered vary between policy providers, so it's important to check the terms and conditions.

The sum assured amount can be level, increasing or decreasing, depending on individual circumstances. A level term policy will pay out a fixed amount whenever death occurs or a terminal illness is diagnosed. Decreasing term assurance is generally cheaper and often used for mortgage protection. The amount of cover, and the premium, reduces in line with the value of the mortgage outstanding. In contrast, some policies can be reviewed with the option to increase the life cover without additional underwriting.

Cover can be on a single or joint life basis. A joint life policy will pay out if one of you dies during the term. There may though be situations where a couple opts to take out separate policies for different amounts of cover; for example, if there are two breadwinners earning significantly different incomes that might need to be replaced.

Another useful feature of term assurance is the option to add waiver of premium cover. For a small additional payment, this ensures that premiums continue to be paid if the policyholder is unable to do so due to long term illness (usually a period of 26 weeks or more).

Term assurance provides cost-effective peace of mind and is a popular solution for younger couples and families when budgets are tighter and there are young children and mortgages to protect.

<u>Family income benefit</u>

Family income benefit, also called family income protection, is a different type of term assurance policy. Rather than pay out a lump sum, family income benefit is designed to provide a regular tax-free income to your family for a set period of time if you die during the term of the plan.

Family income benefit often works out cheaper than term assurance because the monthly income amount would only be paid out for the remaining term, whereas a term policy will pay out the same lump sum, whether that's a few months after the plan starts or a few weeks before it ends.

The suitability of family income benefit versus term assurance is down to individual preference. A large lump sum payout would need to be managed properly to ensure it is invested appropriately and to generate a regular income. On the other hand, you may prefer that your family avoids that stress and instead has the convenience of a monthly income to replace lost earnings.

If a priority is to ensure the family home is safe in the event of your death, taking out a term policy specifically to pay off the mortgage in full would be advisable, rather than arranging a monthly income to service the debt.

Whole of life cover

Unlike term assurance, whole of life insurance lasts for the policyholder's lifetime and will pay out the sum assured to your family whenever you die, as long as you keep paying the premiums. However, the combination of lifelong cover and the guarantee of a cash payout means that whole of life premiums are higher.

On the plus side, once the premium has been agreed, based on factors like your age and health, it remains fixed, making it easier to budget for. Alternatively, you can choose a reviewable premium, which often starts low but is then regularly reviewed by the insurance provider, usually pushing it up.

One important consideration is whether to put the policy in trust. A trust transfers legal ownership of the policy to your chosen trustees and allows you to specify the beneficiaries to whom you want to leave the proceeds. Most whole of life policies are placed in trust. There are two big advantages to doing so. Firstly, the policy proceeds won't be counted as part of your estate when you die, so won't be subject to Inheritance Tax. Secondly, the payout won't have to go through probate, which means your beneficiaries should receive the money sooner. It's important to seek advice on the pros and cons of using trusts.

These advantages mean that whole of life policies in trust are often used for Inheritance Tax planning. As well as providing the security of life cover during your lifetime, the policy will pay out a tax-free sum which is then available to cover any Inheritance Tax liability, keeping your estate intact and avoiding the need for your beneficiaries to fund the tax bill from other sources. Any Inheritance Tax liability needs to be paid before probate can be granted and the estate settled, so this solution provides significant peace of mind for the family and maximises your legacy.

If you are married, any Inheritance Tax liability usually arises when the second person dies. Consequently, whole of life policies used for this sort of planning pay out on the death of the widow or widower.

--

Critical illness cover pays out a tax-free lump sum if you are diagnosed with one of a number of specified illnesses during the term of the policy, such as heart attacks, strokes or cancer.

This could help you and your loved ones meet day-to-day costs and give you the extra breathing space to focus on your own health and wellbeing. Critical illness cover is often put in place alongside life cover to ensure that the family is protected, whatever happens.

The amount of cover you choose will depend on your budget and what expenses you think you might have to cover while you recover or receive treatment. In deciding how long you'd like the cover to last, it's worth thinking about key milestones in your life, such as when your children are no longer financially dependent, when your mortgage is due to be paid off, and when you'll reach state pension age.

Some providers also include dependent children's critical illness cover within a policy, which could be a valuable benefit if you need to take time off work to focus on your child's health.

--

Income protection insurance differs from critical illness cover. Instead of paying out a lump sum, it provides a regular, monthly tax-free income if you are unfit to work for a long period of time due to illness or injury.

Different providers pay out different sums of money, but you can expect to be paid anywhere between 50-70% of your usual gross earnings for the period that you're unable to work.

However, it can take anywhere up to six months to start receiving payments, so you won't receive an immediate cash boost.

Chapter 7: Estate Planning

In my experience, estate planning is one of the most misunderstood areas I discuss with clients. There is still a common misconception that Inheritance Tax (IHT) applies only to the very wealthy. The reality is that the IT professionals I work with who have enjoyed good salaries over the years and invested wisely can easily find themselves drawn into the IHT net. Escalating property values have also played a big part in creating a tax problem for more people.

Of course, discussing our own mortality can be difficult, but the prospect of paying more tax on our wealth when we're gone is a problem that can't be wished away. Every pound that goes to the taxman reduces the legacy you leave to your loved ones. By confronting the issue and making the right plans, my clients get real peace of mind from knowing they've done everything they can to help secure their family's financial future.

So, what is IHT? It's a tax on what you own. These assets can include your family home, any investments you have, family heirlooms and life assurance plans that are not held in trust. The tax is payable on the transfer of assets on death and on certain lifetime gifts.

The current rate of IHT is 40% and it's charged on the part of your estate above the current threshold –

otherwise known as the 'nil rate band' – of £325,000.

There are extra allowances you can claim. If you're passing on a residential property to your immediate family, your executors can claim a further £175,000 (as long as your total estate is worth less than £2 million). This is called the 'residence nil rate band'.

In total, this means that, with the right planning in place, a husband and wife can pass on up to £1 million free of IHT.

There is continuing speculation over whether Inheritance Tax might be abolished. But none of us know what's around the corner and death duties have been around for centuries, so I always stress to my clients that we can only plan based on current legislation and what we know now.

The issue of domicile is a very important one, not just for estate planning but for taxation in general. Domicile is about someone's long-term home. It's a general law concept that transcends residence, nationality and ethnicity. In very broad terms, an individual is domiciled in the UK if they 'belong' in the UK and it is their home.

Domicile has been in the news recently, particularly with regard to the tax treatment of non-UK domiciled residents, who are not liable to pay UK taxes on overseas income and gains unless it's remitted to the

UK. In the Spring Budget in March 2024, the government confirmed that the remittance basis of taxation will be replaced from 6 April 2025 with a residence-based regime under which individuals will not pay UK tax on any foreign income and gains arising in their first four years of tax residence.

The government also announced a consultation on plans to move to a residence-based regime for IHT, which would bring individuals within the scope of IHT on their worldwide assets after 10 years of UK tax residency. This change would not happen before April 2025.

It's an area that requires expert advice. Fortunately, for the very many of my clients who are originally from India or Pakistan, the UK has a favourable tax agreement with both countries that avoids the potential for double taxation and makes planning much easier.

Everyone's circumstances are different and will dictate the appropriate ways to reduce the impact of IHT on your estate. I've detailed below some of the key steps to be considered as part of an effective estate planning strategy.

Write or review your Will

This is always top of my agenda when I meet prospective clients for the first time. Having an up-to-date and legally valid Will is the foundation of sound financial planning, yet it is estimated that over half of UK adults do not have a Will in place.

It is the easiest and most effective way to express the way you would like your wealth distributed when you die. It also includes what funeral arrangements you would like and other wishes, such as who should bring up any dependents. Many clients who come to live and work in the UK are not aware how vital it is to have a Will in place.

Without a Will you are deemed to have died intestate, and your assets will be distributed on your behalf in accordance with the rules of intestacy. This is very unlikely to tie in with your wishes and can be another cause of stress and upset at an already difficult time for your family.

Not having a Will can create other problems. It might mean your estate becomes liable for IHT that might otherwise have been avoided. It will also cause delays in getting probate. A Grant of Probate gives someone the legal right to deal with someone's estate when they die. If a Will exists, it is the executor(s) who applies for probate. If there isn't a Will, the most 'entitled' person can apply to administer the estate, which is normally the closest living relative.

Even with a Will in place, a wait time of up to 20 weeks to get probate is not unusual. Adding further delay will cause more anxiety for your family and prevent them from being able to access your assets when they possibly need them most.

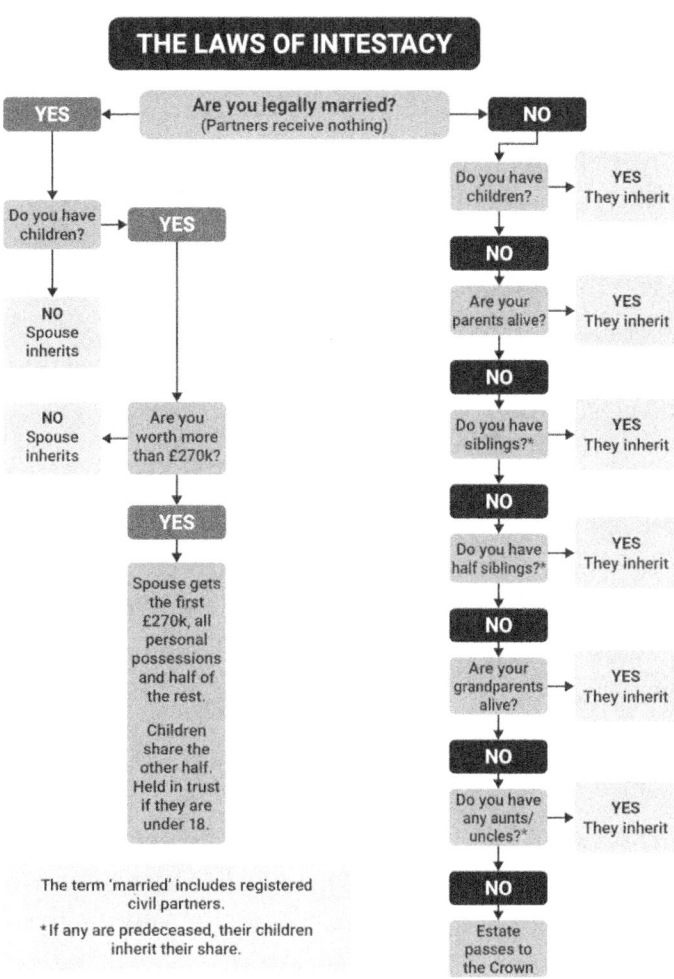

THE LAWS OF INTESTACY

Are you legally married?
(Partners receive nothing)

YES

NO

Do you have children?
YES — They inherit
NO

Do you have children?
NO — Spouse inherits
YES

Are your parents alive?
YES — They inherit
NO

Are you worth more than £270k?
NO — Spouse inherits
YES

Do you have siblings?*
YES — They inherit
NO

Spouse gets the first £270k, all personal possessions and half of the rest.

Children share the other half. Held in trust if they are under 18.

Do you have half siblings?*
YES — They inherit
NO

Are your grandparents alive?
YES — They inherit
NO

Do you have any aunts/ uncles?*
YES — They inherit
NO

The term 'married' includes registered civil partners.

*If any are predeceased, their children inherit their share.

Estate passes to the Crown

Wills are not expensive. You can get a professionally written Will done for a few hundred pounds. I always recommend using a STEP (Society of Trust and Estate Practitioners) qualified solicitor or will writer. This is the top professional qualification for practitioners. There are DIY, off-the-shelf options available, but that does increase the risk of something being incorrect and creating problems further down the line.

The most popular option for couples is a mirror Will, which is essentially identical to the spouse or partner. Typically, that may say that the couple leaves everything to one another and then to their children. Alternatively, a professional will writer will be able to create Wills that allow for individual requests and bequests.

Making a Will is not a once-in-a-lifetime activity. I recommend that Wills are reviewed every three to five years in light of changing circumstances. However, events such as divorce, family bereavement or substantial changes in the value of your assets should be triggers for a more immediate review.

Appoint your power of attorney

Who would look after your affairs if you were unable to? A power of attorney is a legal document that lets you (the donor) appoint trusted people (attorneys) to make decisions about your finances, or your health and care, on your behalf.

I always recommend to my clients that they put in place a power of attorney. In terms of a 'good housekeeping' list, it is up there with sorting out your Will. It isn't a strategy to save IHT but could save you and your loved ones from a huge amount of complication and stress. If you lose the mental capacity to make or communicate your own decisions and don't have a power of attorney set up, it may be necessary for the Court of Protection to become involved.

There are different types of power of attorney and you can set up more than one.

There may be a temporary need for someone to make decisions or act on your behalf, even though you still have mental capacity; for example, if you're in hospital or you might find it hard to get out. In these situations, an ordinary power of attorney will ensure decisions about your financial affairs can still be made.

A lasting power of attorney (LPA) will ensure you're protected in the future if you lose the mental capacity to make your own decisions, or you no longer want to make decisions yourself. There are two types of LPA:

- An LPA for financial decisions covers needs like paying bills, investing money or buying and selling property. It can be used while you still have mental capacity, or you can specify that you only want it to come into effect if you lose capacity.

- An LPA for health and care decisions can only be used once you have lost mental capacity. Your attorney can make decisions about issues such as your medical care, where you should live and what you should eat.

Married couples or those in a civil partnership often assume incorrectly that their spouse will automatically be allowed to make such decisions about their finances or healthcare if they lose the ability to do so. This isn't the case. Without an LPA, they won't have the authority to act on your behalf.

There is standard wording that must be used to set up an ordinary power of attorney, so it's best to get advice from a solicitor or contact Citizens Advice.

To set up an LPA, you can visit the government website (www.gov.uk) to get the necessary forms and for guidance. You can also contact the Office of the Public Guardian (OPG). However, you may prefer to take professional advice from a solicitor if you are unsure about the process or your affairs are more complex.

An LPA must be registered with the OPG before it can be used, which can take up to 20 weeks. There is a registration fee of £82 for each LPA, plus you will need to pay a solicitor's fee if you need their help. It's a small price to pay for significant peace of mind.

Make gifts

Making gifts during your lifetime is an effective and rewarding way to reduce the potential IHT bill your family will have to pay when you pass away. That's because it gives you the chance to see your generosity being enjoyed, and the difference it can make to your loved ones while you're still here.

The rules around lifetime gifting can be complex, so it's an area where it's important to get the right advice. In simple terms, some gifts are exempt from IHT and the value of the gift will immediately fall outside your estate. Larger gifts will typically be exempt after seven years from the date the gift is made. If the donor dies within seven years, the value of the gift is added back into their estate.

There are a number of exempt gifting allowances:

- Individuals have an annual gift allowance of £3,000. This can be one gift or made up of a number of gifts. The allowance can be carried forward to the next tax year, but after that it is lost. That means a couple could potentially gift up to £12,000 in one tax year, which would immediately fall outside their estate. Clients often use this allowance to pass money to grandchildren; for example, to contribute to a Junior ISA to boost their savings for the future. Perhaps it could help them buy their first car or put down a deposit on a new home. Thinking much longer term, it's also possible to pay £2,880 a year into a child's pension, which would be grossed up to £3,600 by basic rate tax relief.

- You can make any number of individual small gifts of up to £250 in any one tax year. The only caveat is that a beneficiary cannot receive a small gift and any of your £3,000 gifting allowance in the same tax year.
- Each parent can give away £5,000 as a wedding gift, whilst grandparents can gift up to £2,500. For anyone else, the tax-free allowance is £1,000.

Some of the more specialised estate planning solutions I offer clients involve the use of trusts and investments, providing ways to reduce the value of an estate and create a fund for beneficiaries, while also allowing an income to be taken. However, these are areas where advice is critical.

Accessibility and affordability are important considerations when it comes to lifetime gifting. Don't give away funds that will be needed to generate the income to maintain your own standard of living. The taxman will 'look through' larger gifts that are deemed to be to the detriment of your own lifestyle.

'Normal expenditure out of income' is another available exemption that needs care. Making a regular pattern of gifts from your income, rather than capital, can be an effective way of removing money from your estate. For example, it could be used to make monthly or annual payments into a savings plan for a beneficiary. Obviously though, what counts as normal expenditure will be down to individual circumstances.

Underpinning any lifetime gifting is the importance of keeping adequate records. When the time comes, it will make the lives of your executors much easier if they have a record of the dates, values and beneficiaries of any gifts.

Save more into a pension

As we've already covered, pensions are a great way to save for retirement, but they can also be a useful estate planning tool as well. Regardless of when you pass away, the money you save into your pension falls outside of your estate, so shouldn't be subject to IHT.

Buy life assurance and put it in trust

We covered earlier the use of life assurance to help you mitigate a future IHT bill. A policy where the sum assured covers any predicted tax bill will greatly reduce the stress on your family. It's essential that the policy is written in trust to ensure the payout falls outside of your estate. Trusts are a vital tool in ensuring the right money goes to the right hands, at the right time.

Chapter 8: The Value of Advice

As I said in the introduction, this is not a DIY guide to financial planning. My aim is to help increase understanding of some of the key areas of personal finance and, in doing so, make people feel more confident about how to achieve financial wellbeing.

Of course, I'd also like to reinforce what I see as the true value of financial advice. Different people will have different reasons for taking advice. For some, it could be to have peace of mind that someone they trust would be there to help their family if they got run over by the proverbial bus.

Naturally, there are some people who don't want advice and maintain that they can do it perfectly well themselves. Often, it's one half of a couple who 'looks after the money' and quite enjoys managing their own investment portfolio. That's fine, but the question they should perhaps ask themselves is what would happen if they were the one to die first? Would their surviving spouse or partner be able to look after their affairs?

What is clear is that, whatever the reason, people who take financial advice are likely to feel more confident, better prepared and more in control of their money.

There is also strong evidence that people who take financial advice are, on average, substantially better off in pensions and other financial assets after ten years compared to those who don't take advice.

I see my role as someone who can make things happen. We can all be guilty of putting things off, particularly the difficult decisions. Partnering with my clients, I can put in place the plan and provide the momentum to ensure those decisions are made and help them navigate a way through life's challenges.

Equally, an adviser can play a vital role in stopping people from making the wrong decisions. Financial decisions driven by emotions such as anxiety and fear rarely deliver good outcomes. An adviser can take the emotion out of decisions and help distinguish noise from useful information.

The benefits of working with an expert financial adviser are incremental, building as the years go by and as you see your plans coming to fruition. Those benefits can have both financial and non-financial value.

The financial advantages are the most obvious, whether that's enabling you to build up a savings buffer, buy a house, or create the big retirement fund that allows you to pack in work early or live later life to the full.

It's also beneficial to have someone who understands the legislation, taxation and technical details that could affect your situation, and how they change over time, particularly in the areas of investments and pensions. Demystifying the rules and regulations is an important and valuable part of an adviser's role.

Yet it is the non-financial benefits that are often underestimated. Reassurance isn't something that can be measured. It is the non-financial value of advice that really makes a difference – having an expert you trust, who can help you as a family and future-proof your financial wellbeing.

You can't put a price on peace of mind.

Testimonials

"Over the last 8-9 years, Rajiv has become an adviser, mentor and supporter. His vision has helped shape our financial future. He has a tremendous understanding of the financial markets and has consistently provided me with holistic financial advice. I wholeheartedly recommend Rajiv due to his exceptional service." Dr Pravin Sangle

"Rajiv has been an invaluable asset to my financial journey. His expertise and dedication have made a significant positive impact on my financial well-being. His consistent communication and willingness to answer my questions have made me feel more confident and secure in my financial decisions." Mr Shami Kandeepan

"Rajiv has been so helpful with advice on everything to do with investments." Mr Neil Abrahamson

"Rajiv has been instrumental in helping me plan and save in the most tax-efficient way. Under his guidance, my retirement portfolio is recovering and growing. I am most grateful for his help." Dr Imtiaz Yusuf

About the Author

Rajiv Prabhakar was born and educated in India, graduating with an honours degree in economics from the University of Delhi and a postgraduate diploma in sales and marketing. After an early career in publishing, he travelled extensively in over 50 countries, before migrating to the UK in the early 80s, where he worked for a multinational IT software company for 20 years.

An opportunity to change career in his mid-50s gave Rajiv the chance to pursue his lifelong interest in finance and economics, qualifying as a financial adviser in 2009. He has since built a successful wealth management practice specialising in the financial planning needs of medical and IT professionals.

Rajiv lives in Rickmansworth and works in London and home counties. He is married to Anshsuta and has a daughter and a son, both medical professionals.

For more information: www.blueoceanwm.co.uk

Acknowledgements

I am grateful to Anshsuta, my wife, who was patient and encouraging whilst I was writing the book.

My inspiration is my children, who have both excelled in their chosen medical professions.

My mother's vision and support was my guiding influence to take up new projects and achieve success.

Finally, thank you to all my coaches, mentors and trainers who have taught me so much.

Printed in Great Britain
by Amazon